THE
HOUSE
THAT
PASTA BUILT

Joe Fresta & Joe Reina

ISBN 978-1-68526-796-4 (Paperback)
ISBN 978-1-68526-797-1 (Digital)

Covenant Books
11661 Hwy 707
Murrells Inlet, SC 29576
www.covenantbooks.com

To J. Kim Tucci

ITALIAN RESTAURANTS

PREFACE

When my wife and friends found out I intended to write a book, they all hesitated and said, "Are you serious?" I told them everyone always asks me how The Pasta House Company came to be. So I decided to sit down and explain how it began.

An old friend, Joe Reina, had just finished writing his first book, *The Goat Sleeps in the Kitchen*, a memoir about his mother, an immigrant from Sicily. He offered to help me write the story. Having grown up on The Hill, the Italian community in St. Louis, Joe knew all the players in The Pasta House story, beginning in 1967 with the Rich and Charlie's restaurant.

I sat down with Joe to discuss what I remembered of the past years. It is really a fairy tale! The partners—Richard Ronzio, Charlie Muggavero, John Ferrara, Joe Fresta, Kim Tucci, Marty Ronzio, and Emil Pozzo, with the exception of Kim Tucci—grew up on The Hill. Kim grew up in North St. Louis. We all had one thing in common, our Italian/Sicilian heritage. The story is a wild one.

The story begins with our authentic Italian/Sicilian culture and how it has impacted our family values and how we have instilled it in our employees.

Our mission early on was to create a family-friendly Italian restaurant, and we set our standard in 1974 when we opened our doors as The Pasta House Company.

Over the past fifty years, we have worked diligently to create an atmosphere that focuses on serving families high-quality food at reasonable prices.

Beyond the in-house dining experience, we have developed programs to "give back" to the St. Louis community, establishing philanthropic values in our culture via our Caring & Sharing Program. Our dedication to family is rooted in all our efforts.

We have had our ups and downs like most success stories. The good news is we have survived.

Join me on this wild and crazy ride. It is proof success can still be found in this great country of ours.

Left to right: Joe Fresta, John Ferrara, Kim Tucci

ITALIAN RESTAURANTS

THE PLAYERS

- Richard Ronzio
- Charlie Muggavero
- John Ferrara
- Joe Fresta
- Kim Tucci
- Marty Ronzio
- Emil Pozzo

Richard Ronzio, as was the case for all the partners, grew up in The Hill in South St. Louis and graduated from Southwest High School. Like most families in the post-World War II era, there was no money for college. Richard had been working all through his four years at Southwest. Most of his jobs were in the restaurants on The Hill. His brother had a pizza restaurant, and he spent a considerable part of his teens flipping pizzas. Upon his graduation from high school, he worked in a factory, Marlo Coil, for a short time. But soon the restaurant business drew him back. His long desire to open his own restaurant was the draw.

Charlie Muggavero, like Richard, attended Southwest High. And he, too, broke into the restaurant business while going to school. His first job at age fifteen was working at Gitto's Pizza on The Hill. Charlie Gitto owned the restaurant, which had been The Isle of Capri, and Charlie Muggavero started there as a busboy. When Gitto took it over, he promoted Muggavero to the kitchen, and he took over making the pizzas at age sixteen. He later worked at Rossini's Pizza, where he gained experience in a more refined Italian restaurant.

John Ferrara attended St. Louis University High School, and his restaurant exposure began at Rossini's Pizza and later at Rinaldi's, which was an Italian restaurant in North St. Louis. Later he went to work at La Chateau, an exclusive private banquet restaurant. It was while attending St. Louis U High that John met Kim Tucci.

Joe Fresta went to school at St. Ambrose Catholic grade school and graduated high school from Christian Brothers College (CBC). He and Charlie Muggavero were boyhood friends. Joe went to work busing tables at Angelo's on The Hill at age fourteen and later held the same position at Ruggeri's. Upon graduation from CBC, he went to work in the family carpentry business. Later, after he married, he purchased his father's pizza parlor and ran the restaurant at night after his carpentry day job.

Kim Tucci graduated from St. Louis University High and went to college at St. Louis University. He was from the downtown Italian neighborhood and, like the rest of the partners, worked his way into the restaurant business while in high school. He decided to teach school after graduating from college, but the restaurant business was calling. He started at the Lombardo's restaurant at age seventeen and later worked at Al Baker's, an outstanding gourmet restaurant in St. Louis. His next venture was acting as the valet manager at Tony's, the upscale restaurant in downtown St. Louis where he ultimately became maître d'.

Marty Ronzio and Emil Pozzo were Richard Ronzio's nephews, and both went to work for Richard and Charlie Muggavero at a very young age when they opened the early Rich and Charlie's restaurants.

Left to Right: Charlie Muggauero, background,
John Ferrara, Unknown Lady, Richard Ronzio

Left to Right: John Ferrara, Kim Tucci

Left to Right: Joe Fresta, Kim Tucci

Sam Garanzini

John Harris, CFO

ITALIAN RESTAURANTS

KEY MEN

- Sam Garanzini, COO: Sam got his experience in the restaurant business early at age twelve busing tables in his uncle's restaurant. He joined the original Rich and Charlie's at age seventeen in November 1967 and worked his way up to his position today and runs The Pasta House restaurants.
- John Harris, CFO: John is from Highland, Illinois, and graduated from St. Louis University with a degree in accounting in 1977. He worked at Alexander Grant, a national CPA firm, from 1977 to 1981 and at Flagg Steel from 1981 to 1985.

    John joined The Pasta House Company in 1985 and has expertly guided the firm through all its turmoils and successes until today.

ITALIAN RESTAURANTS

PROLOGUE

Many books have been written about people who started businesses with little or no money and survived the usual struggles on the road to success. This is not just another "from rags to riches" story.

The meager beginning, evolution, early success, and many failures traverse an unbelievable drama and lead one to believe miracles do happen.

The ups and downs span fifty years. And as the story unfolds, it tests the patience and perseverance of the surviving partners, where most would have given up, thrown in the towel, and walked away.

This was the case for Joe Fresta, John Ferrara, and Kim Tucci, who stayed the course, weathered the storms, and dealt with complicated personalities and the habit of one partner's constant disruption of the business. Finally, when they could no longer tolerate his behavior, they borrowed money to buy him out. The sudden death of one of the founding partners added to the drama in those early years.

The story begins in the 1960s and with the early successes that led to a massive expansion in the 1970s that created extensive bank debt. That debt brought on significant financial stress when interest rates began climbing in the early 1980s as the prime rate reached 20 percent. That followed the request by two of the five partners to be relieved of their personal guarantee on the banknote, putting the burden of the responsibility on Fresta, Ferrara, and Tucci, and again tested their fortitude.

There was no doubt in the minds of the surviving three partners that success was in the future, and their determination against all odds would carry them through the turmoils in those days of woe.

CHAPTER 1

The Hill, the Late 1950s

Without question, one of the most famous neighborhoods in the city of St. Louis is located on the South Side. It is known as the Hill and is an inauspicious twelve-square block section, comprised early on of immigrants from Italy and Sicily. They arrived in the latter years of the nineteenth century and the early twentieth century with barely the clothes on their backs. In those days there was one common denominator among them: they were lower- and middle-class, first- and second-generation people. They lived week to week, and those with any real money could be counted on one hand.

In the 1950s, three restaurants dominated the area: Sala's, Ruggeri's, and Angelo's. All three were primarily steak and Italian food oriented. They employed kids in their teens for the menial jobs, as young as thirteen. Thus, they became the training ground for some of the characters in this story. Such was the case for Charlie Muggavero, Richard Ronzio, Joe Fresta, John Ferrara, Emil Pozzo, and Marty Ronzio. Their ages were all within four years of each other, Richard Ronzio being the oldest. The seventh partner, Kim Tucci, was from the downtown Italian area. His college degree took him on a different path; he became a teacher. Later, he began working at Tony's, a famous restaurant in downtown St. Louis, as a valet parking attendant, soon as a waiter, and finally as maître d'.

1

Tony's at the time was the only five-star Italian restaurant in the United States. It was operated by Vince Bommarito, without question one of the top restauranteurs in the country.

Richard Ronzio went to work there as a busboy in the early 1960s and became the assistant bartender and later the bartender. He brought Charlie Muggavero in initially as a busboy, and he progressed to assistant waiter and later a full-fledged waiter.

About this time, a young immigrant from Rome named Andreino DeSanti arrived on The Hill and married an attractive young lady and, through friends of hers, started working as a waiter assistant at Tony's. Andreino possessed a great personality and was movie-star handsome. He was quickly promoted to waiter status. He developed a clientele all on his own. People, especially women, insisted he serve them.

He was aggressive and strong-tempered and was determined to live the life of the rich and famous. He had no fear and became obsessed with owning his own restaurant.

CHAPTER 2

Andreino's

The largest employer on The Hill was the Magic Chef stove company, formerly called Quick Meal. It was founded in the late 1880s. In the 1950s the firm was running two eight-hour shifts and employed over four thousand employees.

By the early 1960s, the operation moved to Tennessee, and it devastated the employees who were mostly from the Hill.

Several businesses in the surrounding area closed. One of those was a small tavern that served food, primarily at lunch, located directly across the street from the factory. Its clientele were mainly from the stove factory. It was located at the corner of Hereford and Wilson with living quarters above the tavern.

Andreino approached his wife's parents about borrowing money to reopen the tavern. His plan was to open a gourmet Italian restaurant that would rival Tony's. He had their client list and their recipes, and he convinced Richard Ronzio and Charlie Muggavero to join him.

Charlie had his own client list, and Richard knew every customer who frequented Tony's, and he began as the other waiter. Andreino was short of money, and at the opening, he had no funds to buy liquor or wine.

Andreino hired two brothers who were carpenter contractors to remodel the restaurant.

He convinced the local priest at St. Ambrose Catholic Church on The Hill to write an introductory letter about the restaurant to the client lists, and it opened as the only gourmet Italian restaurant on The Hill.

Remember there were three well-known established restaurants mentioned earlier, but they were renowned for their steak menus.

It was an overnight success. Thus begins the story. Charlie Muggavero eventually moved to the kitchen, and Ronzio became the bartender.

A former client from Tony's who loved Richard and Charlie was dining at the restaurant three, sometimes four, nights a week. His name was Bob Webb, a wealthy gentleman from Clayton, a suburb of St. Louis.

Bob had a typical Jewish deli in University City that primarily did takeout.

During the ensuing two years, Andreino's was slammed every night. Reservations were required for Friday/Saturday nights, but unless one had a contact, it could take a month or two to secure a table.

Bob could walk in unannounced and sit at the bar until a table became available. Charlie would cook his favorite meals, at times surprising Bob with delicacies that were not on the menu.

Andreino's wife had an uncle who sat at the top of one of the St. Louis unions. They had an annual benefit for a Catholic saint. And they would bring in Frank Sinatra and Dean Martin, along with an actress named Kay Kendall, to perform.

Andreino would open the restaurant on Sunday exclusively to serve the trio. Sinatra loved the food so much that he requested service in his suite at the Chase Hotel the next two nights, and Charlie Muggavero served them.

Bob Webb took a villa annually in Acapulco and in February 1967 invited both Richard and Charlie to be his guests for two weeks. Let's stop here for a moment. This was a dream. People from the Hill did not travel to resorts like Acapulco, and the thought of staying in a private villa was unheard of.

Andreino would not hear of the two of them taking two weeks off, and a bitter argument ensued. Charlie Muggavero took the lead and said, "We are going."

Andreino told them, "If you go, don't come back. You are fired!"

Charlie and Richard enjoyed the splendor of the renowned Mexico resort and explained to Bob their plight facing them when they returned to St. Louis.

When Bob heard about this, he pleaded with them to take over his deli and introduce the most popular items from the restaurant to the deli menu. They accepted the offer under the condition that they could purchase it and pay him over a period of time, and he agreed. The terms were no cash initially, with a payment due each month based on 100 percent of the net proceeds, to be paid over a three-year period. Rich and Charlie had no money and accepted the offer.

They called Joe Fresta, a carpenter friend of Charlie's, to remodel the place. Again, due to their lack of funds, Joe did the work gratis at night and on weekends. Their longtime friendship prevailed. The place was sixteen hundred square feet that included the small kitchen, which was totally renovated by Joe. It could seat twelve to sixteen people at six tables, which leaned up against the walls. In addition, Joe built two serving counters and a partition wall separating the kitchen. The refrigerator had to be located in the open restaurant. The kitchen was too small to house it.

They named the place Rich and Charlie's. The business was an immediate success. Richard hired his nephews, Marty Ronzio and Emil Pozzo, along with Sam Garanzini, who was seventeen, all kids from The Hill to help run the place. (Sam is with The Pasta House Company as operations manager to this day.) Rich and Charlie had no money to do any advertising, but the throngs of people who frequented the restaurant spread the word early on, and it was warmly accepted based on the fact that the food was good and there were no Italian restaurants in the immediate area. It was primarily a Jewish family-dominated neighborhood. The food was simple old Italian-inspired recipes: pasta with broccoli, toasted ravioli, chunks of chicken breast served on a bed of linguine, and charbroiled salmon with a saffron sauce.

The spaghetti sauce was made with Italian tomatoes, never using tomato paste.

Charlie made a simple old-fashioned salad, made fresh to order.

On Mondays, they offered "All the pasta you can eat," which included salad and garlic bread for $4.95.

The restaurant opened at 4:30 p.m. and closed at 3:30 am. This included Sundays.

This inauspicious start was the beginning of a long journey for the group of friends.

Later, it was decided to open for lunch at 11:00 a.m. and close by 11:00 p.m.

Left to Right at Andreino's
Larry Faust, Jack Benny, Charlie Musgevero

Original Rich & Charlie's

CHAPTER 3

The Trattoria

In 1969 Richard approached Charlie and said, "We are never going to get rich with this deli. Let's open a gourmet restaurant to rival Andreino, but not on The Hill."

Charlie responded, "We have no money to speak of. How do you propose we do that?"

They were buying most of their food—canned tomatoes, parmigiano cheese, etc.—from a company owned by Giovanni Ferrara. And they approached him and his son, John, a waiter at a banquet hall called La Chateau.

Giovanni agreed to invest $35,000 but insisted his son become a partner in Rich and Charlie's, and they concluded the transaction.

Once again Joe Fresta was called on to renovate an existing restaurant that had closed.

They named it The Trattoria, and it opened in early 1970.

John Ferrara later brought his friend Kim Tucci into the fold as a waiter and introduced Kim to Joe Fresta.

Charlie Muggavero moved into the kitchen as head chef and Rich Ronzio as maître d', and John Ferrara and Kim Tucci waited tables. Kim also took on the role of handling public relations.

At this time, Rich Ronzio's two nephews, Marty Ronzio and Emil Pozzo, were running the original Rich and Charlie's, along with Sam Garanzini, the trio being groomed for a future role in the business.

The business ownership was split one-third each between Ronzio, Muggavero, and Ferrara, but dominated by Ronzio.

In late 1969 a second Rich and Charlie's was opened on Woods Mill Road in a St. Louis suburb, and Emil Pozzo took over management of that store. Sam Garanzini took over the management of the original store. This was the early sign of the overall plan by Ronzio to have control of the company, using the nepotism of his nephews.

In 1970 expansion continued, and another Rich and Charlie's opened in downtown St. Louis, and an old friend of the group was hired to manage the store. His name was Charlie Gitto, and he was born and raised on The Hill and brought experience to the table, having operated his own pizza restaurant. He and Charlie Muggavero were well acquainted in that Charlie had worked at Gitto's Pizza as a kid.

What motivates anyone to go into the restaurant business? It is without a doubt one of the toughest. These guys knew how hard it was to achieve success, but it was all they knew.

There was a major difference between Rich and Charlie's and The Trattoria. The Delmar location was old-world in decor, while The Trattoria was well designed and upscale and served a few of the dishes from Delmar but with a more gourmet menu and higher prices and sophisticated dining.

ITALIAN RESTAURANTS

CHAPTER 4

Joe Fresta

My role was building the restaurants, and I was gaining experience running my own pizza restaurant on The Hill. My experience as a carpenter contractor led to a major position in the future growth of the business.

The expansion was placing financial pressure on the business, and a decision was made to seek financing. The partners approached Pioneer Bank and secured a line of credit for $500,000.

In 1971 Emil Pozzo and Marty Ronzio were granted a Rich and Charlie's franchise in South County St. Louis, and it opened with immediate success.

That same year they opened Babe's Barbecue, their first themed restaurant. And later another Rich and Charlie's opened in a suburban shopping center in Crestwood, Missouri.

At the end of 1973 in a weekly meeting, Richard Ronzio suggested bringing all the franchises, along with his nephews, into the fold as one group, for needed management experience. His plan was to expand company-owned stores of Rich and Charlie's across the country along with franchises.

Charlie and his wife, Carol, were preparing to take a long-overdue vacation to Puerto Vallarta, leaving their one-year-old child with Charlie's parents. And Richard's suggestion was tabled until their return.

He and his wife flew from St. Louis to Houston and boarded the plane for their long-awaited vacation to Puerto Vallarta. As the Aeromexico jet approached the airport, it crashed into the jungle twenty-five miles south of the Pacific Coast resort.

Initially, there was no definite word on the fate of the twenty-three passengers aboard the plane. But later it was proclaimed all perished, including the pilots and the rest of the crew members.

The shock of losing a good friend and partner was devastating to the group, and people in The Hill were touched emotionally, especially concerning a baby who would never know his parents.

This put tremendous pressure on the business from the standpoint of Charlie's contribution to the day-to-day operation of the kitchen and also financially because there was no money to buy his third of the business. At the time, Richard Ronzio and John Ferrara owned the other two-thirds of the business.

An offer was made to Charlie's parents on behalf of the child. The offer was refused, and a bitter lawsuit followed. After extensive legal fees, a settlement was reached, and the business was forced to borrow the money to pay both the attorneys and the child's grandparents.

Joe Fresta mulling over plans for a new store

ITALIAN RESTAURANTS

CHAPTER 5

Kim Tucci

My friendship with Kim Tucci was fast becoming what ultimately led to a forty-five-year partnership. We were offered a Rich and Charlie's franchise in late 1973 for a site in Ballwin, Missouri, which cost us $20,000. Neither of us had twenty cents. We needed a loan for it and capital to build the restaurant.

I approached my uncle Sam Caputa, and he loaned us $100,000, and I personally with a contractor friend built the store.

It was 3,600 square feet, located in a strip center. It could seat 136 people. We hired all kids from The Hill to help us run the business.

Kim did an outstanding job of promoting it, all free publicity, and we opened to a huge crowd waiting outside the door the first day. The business was so good that people would be standing outside the door waiting to get in on weekends until eleven at night, an hour beyond our normal closing time.

In a meeting in 1974, Richard Ronzio suggested meeting with our attorneys to combine the businesses under one corporate name to head up all the themed restaurants, and he insisted on renaming Rich and Charlie's under the heading of the new title. We thought this was insane and an expensive decision. All the signs, menus, and decor in the restaurants would have to be changed. But there was no changing his decision.

Our attorneys, Chuck Deaba and Jim Souter, came up with the name The Pasta House Company.

Later, at another meeting, Richard's idea of bringing in his nephews with Kim and me as partners to increase corporate management sounded like a good idea for expansion. At that time, he and John Ferrara owned the shares equally. Richard and John retained 50 percent of the business. Emil Pozzo and Marty Ronzio, Richard's nephews, each received 12.5 percent. Kim and I also received 12.5 percent each; our stores were brought in-house.

While it was never discussed, this gave Richard control over his nephews.

Kim and I saw no problem with the proposal, and we opted for it. Everyone had a role. I was in charge of the construction of new restaurants and was on call for problems and troubles with maintenance. Kim's responsibility was advertising and public relations, Richard's role was expansion and selecting future sites, John Ferrara was president and in charge of operations, and the nephews were to oversee training of future employees and/or franchisees.

The expansion continued in the ensuing years with new company stores and the start of franchises. Company stores under The Pasta House name were established after 1974 in the Crestwood Plaza shopping center, the Northwest Plaza center, and O'Fallon, Missouri, all suburbs of St. Louis. In addition, a themed restaurant called Fred's Fried Chicken was opened in Crestwood.

We opened the Flamingo Cafes, one in Westport and the other on Euclid, a "hot" area near two of St. Louis's major hospitals. That same year we opened the Palm Beach Cafe also on Euclid and the Lido Cafe in Westport.

These restaurants primarily served Mediterranean-style cuisine, along with some of the best-selling items from The Pasta House menu. We opted for the name change because the clientele in the area were wealthy patrons and demanded more exclusive detail in the decor of the restaurants.

Richard Ronzio selected a location in an expensive mall in Houston, Texas, that turned into a fiasco. It was a very expensive build-out, in a bad location. The business never got off the ground floor, and we ultimately closed it. The bailout of that lease cost the firm a tremendous amount of money and caused serious friction with the partners.

We all tried to avoid controversy but could no longer contain ourselves. Kim and I and John Ferrara began discussing buying out Richard. We were reluctant to discuss this with the nephews for obvious reasons. But they, too, were tired of Richard's quest for power and his overall disruption of business affairs. He and John were drawing large salaries; that, too, was bothering us.

The problem facing us regarding the buyout was money. Our debt at the bank by this time was over $1.4 million, and the interest was mounting each month. It was 1980, and we were paying two points over the prime rate, which was 8 percent. We worked with our bank regarding what we could borrow to pay Richard.

During the discussion, we also showed a five-year plan for company-owned stores and franchise cities we were considering, along with the expansion of some of the themed restaurants.

After several meetings, they agreed to extend the line of credit an additional $750,000!

We had decided to build a commissary to do all the preparations for the stores at one location.

We began importing containers of pasta, cheese for grating, and large cans of tomato sauce directly from Italy. We also started making our own ravioli and cannelloni.

John Ferrara came up with the idea of approaching the large grocery stores to see if they were interested in doing a test for our sauces, ravioli and cannelloni, and it worked.

Dierbergs, Schnucks, and Shop 'n Save jumped in and placed our products in all their stores.

This really enhanced our bottom-line profits and continues today to be a moneymaker for the company.

Fresta-Tucci original Franchise store in Ballwin, Missouri

CHAPTER 6

The Buyout, Richard Ronzio

John Ferrara opened a meeting on Monday, April 14, 1980 (I will never forget it). And we broke the news to Richard that we wanted to buy him out. Both his nephews attended, and John did not mince any words!

Richard was aghast. He shouted at us, "You ungrateful idiots, you forget I started this whole thing!"

The ranting and screaming continued with every swear word one could imagine. We were ready for it, and we allowed the expected boisterous retard to John's calm words to finally end.

With that, John asked, "Are you finished? Come on, Richard. We have all been dealing with stress. We all own the company. We all are experiencing debt as a result with regard to decisions on bad locations that you put us into. This business is supposed to operate as a democracy. It is not your business; it is our business. We are prepared to make you a cash offer, which we don't have. That will force the company to go deeper into debt. Think about a number that will make you happy, and let's stay friends."

There was limited discussion from him after his outburst. I truly believe to this day he went into shock and was speechless.

We had many locations being considered for company expansion, which we tabled pending Richard's decision. For the next ten days, he failed to show up at the office. We assumed he was with an attorney and an accountant working on a final number.

We were preparing our number. John Ferrara was handling the entire procedure. Kim and I were in the dark. We did not know what the hell was going on, nor was John discussing it with us. We had such small-percentage ownership. Our opinion on the matter was not being considered, but John knew we agreed with the buyout.

John met privately with Richard and agreed to pay him $500,000 and signed the agreement and paid him. Kim and I were never apprised of how the deal was handled as to Richard's stock. The $500,000 increased the bank loan to a little over $2 million!

We learned later it increased John Ferrara's overall percentage to 50 percent. Ronzio's stock went to him.

There was relief in the fact that Richard was gone, and a dark cloud lifted over us. We felt we could now proceed with the planned expansion, both company-owned stores and themed restaurants.

At this time, we had an attorney by the name of Jim Souter and a CFO named Bernie Wagner. They were directing us. We knew the restaurant business but little about administration and the formal end of running a business. We also had no idea of what was in store for us with regard to interest rates, and by the end of 1980, the rates had doubled. We were paying 18 percent interest, and reality struck.

Earlier in the year, Kim Tucci was diagnosed with prostate cancer. After enduring painful postoperative treatment, he returned to work.

CHAPTER 7

Financial Problems

1981 remains one of my worst years in the restaurant business. Our bank debt had climbed to $2.6 million, and we were paying 22 percent interest. We had signed personal guarantees on the loan. Our interest payments were running $48,000 a month, and the daily receipts barely took care of it and the general overhead. There was nothing left for us. The day-to-day stress was keeping me awake at night.

At our weekly meeting, Emil Pozzo and Marty Ronzio asked to be released from the loan at the bank in exchange for their ownership. And once again John Ferrara stepped in and handled the situation, severing their ownership, giving each of them a store in South County St. Louis. That left the three of us holding the bag on the debt.

The high interest rate carried into 1982. And we got what was to be a major break. A good customer by the name of Richard Pisani walked into the Delmar original store one day and began talking to Sam Garanzini who was the store manager about a firm he owned that specialized in directing companies to franchising. I was working on a banged-up door in the kitchen and overheard the conversation and sat with Rick and listened to his pitch. I concluded the conversation and told him I would discuss it with John and Kim.

We met with Pisani and his partners, Mike Clayton and Steve Caby, and signed an agreement with them to handle the franchises. The name of their firm was the American Marketing Company. Again our lack of sound business experience surfaced, for as part of the deal they received 2 percent of the 5 percent we received from the franchise fees paid.

Kim placed an ad in the newspaper as a test, and we received over three hundred responses.

We had a small themed store in a well-to-do area in West St. Louis called Little Ernie's and converted it to a The Pasta House Company store. Pisani brought a client for it and enlisted him as the first official franchisee. His name was Dave Ruth. His fee was 5 percent of the gross receipts, in addition to the franchise fee. In the ensuing years, we sold an additional twenty-three franchises with American Marketing.

Our good luck continued with the election of Ronald Reagan, who was sworn in as the fortieth president of the United States on January 20, 1981. He was a conservative Republican having served as the governor of California and was a well-known Hollywood actor.

He inherited an economic mess from the previous administration. Unemployment reached 8.5 percent in 1981 but later went to 10.8 percent in 1982. Inflation was running like a wild horse and was out of control and reached 8.9 percent, but in some parts of the country, it ran over 12 percent.

Reagan surrounded himself with some of the finest financial minds of the country. He was able to convince the Federal Reserve to lower the prime rate to 10 percent in early 1982. He pushed Congress to pass major income tax reductions across the board for all Americans, which lowered the high rate of 70 percent to 28 percent.

In addition, as part of the tax plan, he zeroed in on the weak areas in the economy by inserting tax incentives to kick-start them. New construction of commercial buildings was given 15 years to depreciate (previously it was 40 years). It could be depreciated 50 percent in the first five years once they were under operation. This really helped us reduce our taxes on new buildings we were purchasing for the stores we were building.

For the first time in nearly three years, John, Kim, and I were able to pay ourselves a livable salary. And we could breathe. We revived our old expansion plans and aggressively went after franchise clients in key markets where there was little competition for our concept.

CHAPTER 8

1982, Sam Garanzini

The recovery brought new confidence to us. Interest rates dropped substantially, and we renewed expansion. John Ferrara was juggling many balls: the day-to-day running of the restaurants, financial matters, administration, the commissary sales to the grocery stores, and personnel. Kim was helping him a little, but those tasks were too much for them.

I was busy with new store construction and maintenance and lacked experience in the role they were playing. The truth of the matter was none of us had the knowledge to run a large restaurant business.

In 1978 Sam Garanzini was running our store in the Frontenac shopping center and had been with us since Rich and Charlie's opened. He knew the operation as well as any of us, and we decided to bring him to corporate as vice president of operations.

Initially, we gave Sam seven stores to operate and later increased it to fourteen. By this time, between company-owned stores and franchises and the themed restaurants, it became too much for him. And we brought in two more individuals, John Marciano and Frank Puleo, to assist Sam. Frank was in charge of directing the chefs and doing the recipes. John was responsible for store operations and assisted Sam regarding personnel.

Little did we know selecting Sam for his new role at corporate was to be a lifetime responsibility. There was no doubt he had the passion, integrity, and determination to help us build the business. We were just so immersed in our own day-to-day responsibilities and growing so rapidly that there was no time to think long-term. We felt it was time to strike while the business was hot and continue the winning hand.

Sam became an integral part of the company. He implemented consistency in how we cooked pasta sauces by making "butter balls," which included various ingredients in each ball for different sauces. This made it easier for the cooks to get the pasta to the table quicker and more efficiently, thus enabling us to turn the tables quicker.

Sam controlled prices for food and liquor, and he helped increase our profits in both areas.

Next, he created incentives for the employees to help increase service to the customers.

But Sam saw above and beyond and requested franchises of his own. We saw this as a testimony of his desire to be part of the growth, and we welcomed granting him six locations over the years.

His loyalty, hard work, and dedication turned out to be one of the best decisions we ever made, for he has graduated to COO and runs the business today, over fifty years since his first day at the original Rich and Charlie's!

In 1980 we opened a Pasta House restaurant in the Galleria, a high-end shopping center, in Richmond Heights, a suburb of St. Louis. That same year we issued a franchise for a store in Chesterfield, a suburb of St. Louis.

There were numerous requests for franchises, and it was keeping John busy interviewing prospects and Kim occupied with advertising and public relations and me with new store construction and maintenance.

In 1982 we opened a franchise on DeBaliviere on the far west end of the city not far from Washington University. It attracted large crowds for lunch and evening dining and entertaining. That same year we sold a franchise for a store in another high-traffic area on Dorsett Road in a high-income suburb west of the city.

Mike Shannon

I was very close to Mike Shannon, the former third baseman for the St. Louis Cardinals baseball team. At this time, he was doing color broadcasting for the Cards. We were boyhood friends, and his popularity among the St. Louis fans was outstanding. I went to high school with Mike who was an outstanding athlete, excelling in all sports, including football.

While at the University of Missouri on a football scholarship, he was approached by the St. Louis Cardinals baseball team and signed a contract at age nineteen. He went on to become a star player for the team and retired a Cardinal.

We had discussed opening a restaurant at one time while he was still playing.

We went to lunch, and I proposed doing a themed restaurant using his name for the restaurant and specializing in his favorite foods.

He agreed, and I took the concept to John and Kim, and they welcomed the idea. By the end of the year, we opened Mike Shannon's with an agreement to pay him a royalty of 5 percent of the gross revenue.

I became involved with a man named Bill McDermont who had experience in restaurant design, and with Mike's help and extensive Cardinals baseball memorabilia, we came up with a well-designed store.

Bill went on to become an integral part of the logo and design team for the company.

We located it right next door to the Cardinals stadium, and it caught the crowd before the games and those exiting it. The restaurant opened with amazing fanfare. Kim did an excellent job on advance publicity and continued the hype through the media after the opening. It was filled to capacity every night, with an hour wait to be seated, especially when there was a game.

The success of Shannon's later led to additional celebrity restaurants.

Perhaps our naïveté was the benefit of who we were, for we quickly forgot the trauma of the early 1980s and the insane interest we were paying on the debt. We aggressively continued expansion in 1983 and 1984, which was increasing debt at the bank.

We sold franchises for a store on Gravois in South St. Louis and another in High Ridge in suburban St. Louis. We went out of the city and opened another franchise in Cool Springs, Tennessee. Kansas City opened with a bang the same year.

In 1984, we put a franchise in Paducah, Kentucky, and another in Springfield, Missouri.

We took a booth at the franchise show at the St. Louis convention center that year and sold three to a group from Florida. I remember it well, for I spent quite a bit of time there building those stores.

Money was rolling in. We were charging a minimum of $45,000 per franchise and 5 percent of the gross receipts annually.

We had weathered the storms—economic problems, high interest rates, those with former partnerships, the buyout of Richard Ronzio, and the death of Charlie Muggavero. A presence was taking place in St. Louis beyond any the three of us ever dreamed. Kim had done an excellent job on public relations. We were dubbed "The Pasta House boys."

We decided to change our logo, and it was suggested we contact a top firm in Chicago named Cooper Design. After reviewing many concepts, we finally settled and used a red tomato in the background and the three of us wearing chef hats at the top, and it changed The Pasta House lineage.

During the year we were approached by a company called Miller & Sons Catering to purchase our commissary business, and we agreed to sell it for $1.5 million with $750,000 as a deposit. The decision to accept the offer was because we were at our limit regarding the loan at the bank and we needed the money to continue expansion. Later Miller failed to acquire a bank loan for the balance, and they walked from the deal. Their deposit stayed with us.

Mike Shannon's

C H A P T E R   9

1985, John Harris

Our accountant, Bernie Wagner, decided it was time to retire. John Ferrara approached our accounting firm and asked them to find us a new CFO. And after interviewing a few prospects, we hired John Harris, one of the best moves we ever made for he started in 1985 and holds that position today.

We had no idea what a mess our accounting department was in, but we hired the right man to clean it up. John, Kim, and I were not financially educated and knew little about the accounting end of the business. John Harris took control and stabilized that part of our business.

During the year we opened a store called The Clocktower in a shopping center on the far northwest part of the city. We sold franchises for Springfield, Missouri; Bloomington, Illinois; Branson, Missouri; and Evansville, Indiana. In addition, Sam Garanzini took a franchise for Fairview Heights, a suburb of St. Louis.

The wild expansion continued in 1986 and 1987 with company stores opening on Lindbergh Boulevard and Highway 55 in a shopping center and another in the Northwest Plaza shopping center. There were franchise openings in Alton, Illinois, and Springfield, Illinois.

We showed nice profits in 1986 and 1987, and the three of us took nice salaries and bonuses.

In 1987 the Cardinals won the National League pennant and played the World Series against the Minnesota Twins, and during home games, the business at Shannon's was insane. We ran out of food every game.

That same year President Reagan met with Mikhail Gorbachev, the leader of Soviet Russia, and pledged cooperation to reduce nuclear arms. And this reduced tension between our country and theirs.

Inflation held steady, but there was a jump in interest rates. It went to 7.5 percent. John Harris warned us to be careful regarding the growing debt at the bank.

In 1988–1989 we opened in Florida with franchises in Tampa and Clearwater. Sam Garanzini, with partners Frank Ferrara (John's brother) and Frank's son Frank Junior, opened another in Carbondale, Illinois. There was a state university there, and the students helped make it a success. We also opened a franchise store in St. Petersburg, Florida.

By this time Sam Garanzini had taken over running the day-to-day operations, working with the chefs, designing methods to shorten the cooking process to get food to the table. This helped us to turn the tables faster at the restaurants. With him at the helm of the operation and John Harris handling administration and accounting, it gave John Ferrara the time he needed handling expansion. Kim had the time to handle advertising and public relations and I to do construction and maintenance. We were on a roll.

The economy favored us. Unemployment had leveled off since the early part of the decade. Business was so good that the memory of the bank debt and the struggles with 22 percent interest was no longer nagging us.

But the success was short-lived. The moments of despair surfaced once again. The *Challenger* spaceship explosion had a temporary slowdown in business as was the hijacking of Pan Am Flight 73, in Karachi. And the same minor interruption occurred when the TWA bombing happened on a flight blowing a hole on the side of the plane that sucked four passengers out. But the disasters soon stopped, and overall they had little impact on our business for the year.

President Reagan's reduction of income taxes did have a major effect because it was across the board for all taxpayers. Overnight our daily increases were astounding.

In 1987 President Reagan traveled to Berlin and made a historical speech at the Berlin Wall that separated communist-controlled East Berlin from West Berlin since the end of World War II.

He asked Gorbachev to tear down the wall, which he later did.

For the better part of the year, we enjoyed the fruits of our hard-earned work, but it was not to last. Another hurdle showed its ugly face for on October 19 the stock market crashed and the Dow dropped 22 percent and panic prevailed.

The bear rose from a dead sleep, and the long ride of the bull had ceased. It had an immediate effect on our business. We decided to take a serious look at the expansion plans we were considering. The 1980 lesson was embedded deeply in our minds.

1988 was an election year, and it dominated the press. Vice President George Bush won the Republican nomination, he ran virtually unopposed, and the Democrats nominated the governor of Massachusetts, Michael Dukakis, to run against Bush.

Dukakis was well known on the East Coast, but not nationally. He was a veteran and a Harvard graduate.

Bush was a well-qualified candidate for the White House, having served as a Navy pilot in World War II, an ambassador to the United Nations, and as the head of the CIA. He was elected in November unanimously and was sworn in on January 20, 1989.

His election calmed things down with regard to the nation as a whole, and things returned to normal in the economy.

We opened franchises in Palm Harbor, Florida, toward the end of the year and a themed restaurant called Zia Mia in Bethesda, Maryland.

ITALIAN RESTAURANTS

CHAPTER 10

1989

The economy continued to favor us; unemployment dropped to 5 percent, the lowest in sixteen years; the stock market recovered; and we once again began expansion. I was concerned about the growing drug problem in the nation, especially the increased use of cocaine. It was widely used, no longer in the underprivileged neighborhoods. The federal government was spending millions trying to stop the spread, but it was like a ruptured dike. Every time they caught a large drug lord and made a significant "bust," another source found its way into the country.

In 1990, Kim approached his friend Charlie Spooner, the famed coach of the St. Louis University basketball team, about opening another celebrity restaurant. And he agreed.

We put the same deal together we had with Mike Shannon, giving him 5 percent of the gross sales.

At the time a shopping center had been developed in what was formerly the Union railway station near downtown St. Louis, and we opened the store in it. It was an overnight success because during the off-season Charlie followed the same pattern Mike Shannon did and showed up greeting people who were dining.

With the success of Shannon's and Charlie Spooner's, Kim took advantage of his relationship with the owner of the St. Louis

Blues hockey team and met with Brett Hull, the star of the team, and engaged him to enter an agreement to open a restaurant.

The enticement was the 5 percent royalty for use of his name. Part of the deal was his participation in greeting people dining during the off-season.

We opened that store in a nice shopping center in a high-end area on Olive Street Road in Chesterfield, Missouri, west of the city.

The continued good news of the year was interrupted by US Armed Forces entering Kuwait and driving the Iraqi military force out of the country in what was called Desert Storm, stopping just outside the Iraq border.

We sold another franchise and opened a store in Clearwater, Florida, continuing our spread across that state. All this expansion continued to increase profits.

I always wanted to get my sons, Joe and Paul, into the business. And we put them to work initially in the commissary. I wanted them to learn the business from the ground floor up. Some of my friends warned me it was not a good plan to go into business with your kids.

We put one on the truck to deliver food to the restaurants, and the other worked on food preparation in the kitchen and also part-time in the office.

Later they worked as waiters in the stores and also washed dishes and experienced cooking.

Soon I sat with them to see where their heads were. The last thing I wished to do was force them to stay in the business. Joe opted to leave and went to work for Coca-Cola as a salesman. Paul stayed on for a while. And finally he, too, left to follow his own career in real estate.

There was a slowdown in 1991. Things at our themed store Zia Mia in Washington, DC were not going well, and we decided to close it to stop the money drain. We bought out the remainder of the lease, and it eroded the year's profit, and we ended the year in the red.

In 1992 we opened a franchise store in O'Fallon, Missouri. We also opened an additional store in Springfield, Illinois. Those franchise fees helped us show a profit for the year.

This was another election year, and George Bush was running against an upstart Democrat from Arkansas, William Jefferson Clinton. The press favored Bush. But as the year progressed, Clinton was gaining ground pressuring Bush, because he had raised taxes after claiming he wouldn't when he ran against Dukakis in 1988.

This had alienated conservative Republicans, and another wealthy Texan entered the race as an independent candidate by the name of Ross Perot. He, being an astute conservative businessman, offered an alternative to both Bush and Clinton. He was doing well by June with many states favoring him. But by the end of July, he dropped out, opening the door for Clinton who was a provocative speaker, drawing massive crowds.

In November Clinton defeated George Bush in a landslide victory taking thirty-two states. Our business had a nice rebound, and 1992 showed a nice profit.

Clinton was sworn in on January 20, 1993, as the forty-second president of the United States.

That year ushered in the power of the oil cartel in the Middle East. The price of oil dropped dramatically.

The World Trade building was bombed without serious damage, but it shook the country. There was no doubt we were vulnerable to terrorism, and the CIA got seriously involved, zeroing in on suspected terrorist individuals.

The evolvement of Web browsers popularized the use of the Internet and the wide use of home computers.

Money was easily available, especially venture capital, and IPOs were the talk of the stock market for growth in all matters related to dot-coms that dominated firms related to the Internet. Some of these startups had never earned a profit, but it did not stop the gullible patrons of the stock market from gobbling up the stock.

It was only a matter of time for the "bubble" to burst, which it did. The market dropped substantially, and the country went into another recession. Due to the negative economy, we held back opening any new stores. Our business once again nosedived, and we were forced to close some of the stores, which included Brett Hull's. It was the worst. Buying out the lease cost us close to $1 million!

JOE FRESTA & JOE REINA

In 1994 we stayed the conservative course. Unemployment had crept up and reached 6.2 percent, and the prime rate jumped to 7.25 percent and was hampering our profits. Business at our downtown restaurants slowed because the baseball players went on strike and the season ended with no World Series. However, by taking a conservative stance, watching food costs, reducing advertising, and putting a hold on pay increases, we showed a profit for the year.

In 1995 we sold a franchise to a couple from Farmington, Missouri. But the excitement was overshadowed by the bombing of the federal office building in Oklahoma City. A total of 168 people lost their lives to what initially was thought to be an outright terrorist group.

The FBI got involved in the investigation. It was learned that a bomb inside of a truck caused the explosion. Over twenty thousand interviews were conducted, and forty thousand investigation leads were carefully scrutinized.

A police artist did a sketch of a person believed to be in the immediate area of the building, which later led to the arrest of Timothy McVeigh, who was in jail at the time for carrying a concealed weapon. He was accused of the bombing along with his coconspirators, tried, and convicted.

In 1996 the economy recovered, and unemployment dropped to 5.1 percent, the lowest in eight years. This prompted the stock market to kick in the afterburners, and the Dow rose to an all-time high. The roller coaster continued its ride.

We kept a conservative profile and agreed to hold off further expansion with the thought of reducing our debt at the bank. We increased our salaries and reduced the stress we had been living with for years.

The new store on South Lindburgh

ITALIAN RESTAURANTS

CHAPTER 11

1997

Our financial situation continued to improve, thanks to the guidance of John Harris. The team on the operation side with Sam Garanzini and his management staff was so well organized there were times John, Kim, and I had little to do from an operation standpoint.

We were blessed with a strong economy and low unemployment. It reached 4.6 percent. The stock market hit an all-time high and doubled in the past two-and-a-half years.

We continued our conservative approach with no new store openings.

We elected to sell Mike Shannon's to Mike and a partner; our agreement with him ended on a positive note. We finalized the sale with Mike and showed a $400,000 profit.

Kim and I decided to close some of the themed restaurants for business had slowed considerably. Then Charlie Spooner passed away, and we closed that store and sold the lease to Panera Food.

1998 was a good year. Unemployment continued to drop; it was at 4.3 percent at the end of the year. We closed the store in Columbia, Missouri. It was bleeding money, but it had no impact on the year's profit, and we ended up with another profitable increase in sales and profit for the year.

John Ferrara received an inquiry from a couple in Sacramento and sold two franchises to them. The two stores opened simultaneously and tied me up for almost six months, and they did well initially.

I was fortunate to be close to Palm Springs, and my buddy Joe Reina invited me down for a weekend to relax and play golf.

We kept waiting for the next disaster to strike. I was in the stock market and doing well; some months I made more in the market than my salary from the company.

The Cardinals had traded for Mark McGwire from the Oakland Athletics, and he broke Roger Maris's home run record, and the stadium was at full capacity every game.

After my time in Sacramento, I had a lot of time on my hands and started playing golf, and the three of us began taking time off to enjoy the fruits of our labor. This continued through 1999.

2000

John Ferrara had been gaining weight, a lot of weight. He went to a doctor who specialized in stomach bypass operations and informed us he was going to have the procedure and needed some time off to recover. Kim and I tried in vain to talk him out of it. He refused to listen and had the operation, and shortly thereafter, he got a serious infection caused by internal bleeding.

Sadly, John passed away at his home in Creve Coeur at age fifty-four.

He was admired for his zest for life. His longtime friend George Westfall said, "John enjoyed the good life and was rarely down, regardless of conditions that were impacting his life."

He was well known for his ability to cook and loved to cook and entertain people.

He was eager to utilize his time and volunteered for many causes, such as cancer and AIDS research, and donated money to his favorite hospital, St. Jude.

John handled our keyman insurance and failed to increase the value of the business with regard to the payout in the event one of us should die. As a result, after he passed, to settle with his estate, we were $770,000 short with the insurance payout, forcing us to borrow the money—another financial trauma.

Kim elected to take on John's responsibilities as president. It was down to the two of us. There were days when I would go back over the years and wonder how we reached this point. All the trauma and stress caused me to sit back and think of the early days and how we survived. I asked myself, "Why? Why did it end up like this?" I was a carpenter, a kid from The Hill. I worked at Angelo's and bussed tables at age fourteen. Later, I did the same at Ruggeri's. After I married Phyllis, I was running my pizza restaurant at night after working all day as a carpenter. I was content, making good money at both, with little or no debt, no stress, and no partner problems.

But here I was. There was no going back. The good news was I was healthy and our business was good, and that erased the mood.

Later in the year, the two restaurants in California fell on bad times due to bad management and insufficient cash for the franchisees to weather the storm, and we were forced to close them. To walk from the leases, we lost close to $1 million!

When I received the news from John Harris on what those leases cost us, I again drifted back to the past. I thought about all the restaurants I had built across the country. And here I was, sixty-one years old. Where did the last thirty-three years go? It seemed like yesterday Charlie Muggavero called me and asked if I could make some minor renovations at the original Rich and Charlie's on Delmar.

They had no money, and I did the improvements gratis; they did feed me. It was no big deal. That's what friends are for. I asked myself if I would do it again had I known what I was getting into.

Most guys my age would be thinking of retiring. That is the last thing I was going to do. Our business was good. Kim and I had become good friends. He would handle major problems. "Don't worry about it, Joe. I will take care of it." He had to deal with those stress-related incidents.

It was our turn, Sam had operations under control, and John really had the financial part handled.

We received an inquiry from a group in the Dominican Republic regarding information about a franchise there. They wanted two initially, and we signed them up. I went there and built the two restaurants, and both opened in 2000. Later they wanted to open a third in 2001, and we granted it. The $45,000 franchise fees were feeding our profits. The same was true for the 5 percent royalty fees. Despite the money we paid John Ferrara's estate, we showed a profit for the year.

In 2001 we also sold two franchises for openings at the St. Louis Lambert airport.

We were in the wrong part of the airport, and business was disappointing. The same thing was happening to our regular business. Some stores were doing well, but others were dragging them down. Kim and I decided to cut some of the management staff.

John Marciano, Sam's assistant, left. And we moved Roger Bastar over to help him. He had been with the company for fifteen years, so there was no loss with regard to Marciano's departure.

Prior to John Ferrara's death, we were building two restaurants in Tennessee. The locations were picked by John and a St. Louis realtor named Mark Zoren.

The restaurants opened in 2001 and closed in 2003. The locations were horrendous, and the losses mounted from day one. The closing cost us $2 million! We sued Zoren for sticking us with the locations and lease buyouts. He and the shopping center management had given us false projections, and we won the case. I sometimes felt like a billiard ball with these financial disasters, bouncing from one cushion to another.

We were holding our own in the early part of the year. George W. Bush was sworn in as the forty-third president on January 20, 2001. Little did we know the turmoil coming.

We opened Joe's Chili Bowl, and it was met with immediate success. We did a franchise store in Mt. Vernon, Illinois, and a company store in Creve Coeur, a wealthy suburb of St. Louis.

After severing our relationship with American Marketing, franchising slowed, and we felt the economy played a part in it. We decided if we were going through the trouble of building the store, training the people, and doing all the sub-management, it was better for us to own the store.

The new stores kept me occupied for the better part of the year. We planned to open Creve Coeur in September. We were ready, the help were trained, Sam Garanzini had his group well organized, and Kim spent a great deal of time on public relations heading for a great opening.

Then on September 11, the bombing of the World Trade Center and the other two hijacked plane crashes devastated us. Our concern about the opening was shelved immediately.

It seemed like the world came to a halt. We were lost. Everyone was glued to the TV screen.

This kind of thing did not happen in the United States. We were stunned, business slumped, and the stock market closed. It did not open until the seventeenth of September.

We finally opened Creve Coeur with little fanfare, and it took a few weeks before business picked up.

It did not take President Bush and his vice president, Dick Cheney, long to react. And the war with Afghanistan took effect as a result of the bombings. The invasion happened on October 7. The country's war machine went into action, and because of it, unemployment continued to drop. Our business picked up by mid-October, and we cautiously began exploring areas to expand.

From 2002 to 2004 we had trouble finding areas that suited us for expansion. We spent a serious amount of time searching markets outside Missouri and Illinois. There was a heavy concentration of either Italian restaurants or other chains, such as Carrabba's and Olive Garden, that dominated the areas. There was nothing that grabbed me and Kim, and we elected to stay put.

We lost money in 2003 and 2004, and once again, it was difficult to keep our heads up. I continued to wonder was it all worth it.

1989 City of Hope, Men of the Year
Standing Left to Right: Joe Fresta, Kim and Sharon Tucci
Seated Left to Right: Phyllis Fresta, Kathy and John Ferrara

John Ferrara and Joe Fresta

CHAPTER 12

2005 continued the struggle, but we kept looking for opportunities. We found a great location in Chesterfield, a beautiful suburb of St. Louis, and opened a store there. It was an overnight success. Later we were offered a great lease to open a store in the Galleria, a well-designed enclosed mall in Clayton, and opened a store there. The good news was despite the expense of building those two stores, we showed a small profit for 1995. The economy began to show serious promise for the future.

In 2006 the economy continued its robust growth. Kim and I were living the dream. I long wished to belong to a fine country club and joined a small club in North St. Louis. I had been a guest at numerous clubs around the city, but this was my chance to pay back my friends for their generosity by having them as guests at my club.

The stock market continued to be good for me, the Dow Jones opened at 11,409, and Phyllis and I were enjoying life to the max. We continued our lifelong ambition to see the world and traveled abroad and returned to Italy in May.

The business was reaching all-time highs. Sam Garanzini had designed methods to cut the preparation time in the morning at the stores, which literally helped reduce our early morning staff. John Harris was reducing our bank debt, and Kim and I were getting awards for excellence in the restaurant business.

Because of the efforts of Sam and John, there were days Kim and I would arrive in the morning, check on the prior day's receipts, and go for an early lunch or head for the golf course, content to know everything was under control.

We were bringing in forty-foot containers of pasta and parmigiano cheese from Italy, and we became the largest importer of both as an independent restaurant in the country! This direct buying eliminated the middle man and increased our profits.

The St. Louis Cardinals were on fire, and the stadium was filled to capacity every game. They won the division and later defeated the Texas Rangers in the World Series.

The highlight of the year was the stock market. The Dow closed at a record-high 12,463!

In 2007 I continued putting money in the stock market. It rose to record levels. The Dow opened early at 13,178, and my stocks were rising with it. Kim and I were keeping our eyes open, searching for locations to open more stores.

Unfortunately, not all the franchises were prospering. Sometimes it was the location, and at times it had to do with the franchisee. We were forced to close the store in Jacksonville, Florida.

While the war in Iraq and Afghanistan continued, it was having no effect on our business. It did however capture the news every night.

Carrabba's opened two stores in the St. Louis suburbs, but they had no ill effects on us, and they closed two years later. We were offered a ridiculous lease opportunity for their store in O'Fallon, Missouri, outside of St. Louis. We took advantage of the offer. I remodeled it, and it was an immediate success. That store is still open today.

We became concerned about the war in Iraq when President Bush sent 21,500 troops there. Meanwhile, there was an escalation in the war in Afghanistan. It was hard to understand since there was no proof that either country had had anything to do with the bombing of the World Trade Center or the other two hijacked plane crashes.

We had inquiries from two prospects seeking franchise information, one interested in a location in Union, Missouri, and another for a store in Festus, Missouri, not far from the city. We had no stores in either location, so we began having discussions with both individuals with planned openings in late 2008 or early 2009.

Sam Garanzini approached us about opening a franchise store in Edwardsville, Illinois. And since we did not have a store there, the three of us took a ride to search for a location and granted the franchise to him. He deserved it for the hard work, dedication, and all the years he worked with us. The store was scheduled to open sometime in 2008.

On February 26, the market dropped 416 points. But in July, the Dow rebounded and hit an all-time high and went over 14,000!

I got a scare in August. The market again dropped 387 points on the ninth, and my broker assured me to sit tight, not to be concerned.

My friend Joe Reina and I had a discussion about it and the economy as a whole. He warned me to be careful. A "mess" was coming. He feared interest rates were climbing and that the insane rise in real estate prices was a bubble that was going to burst as was the case in the past with the "dot-com" that threw the country into a recession.

I received a second call from Joe Reina, and he said, "Joe, I got out of the market in October of 2005 and put all my real estate up for sale and decided to ride out the storm. Be careful. Don't be doing any major expansion until we see what happens. Interest rates are climbing, and I believe you will see a peak in '08 with the prime at 8.5–9 percent."

As it turned out the market held its own, and things calmed down by the end of the year. The Dow closed at 13,204, up slightly from the opening the first of the year. Once again my broker advised me to relax, and I did.

The company showed a great profit for the year, alleviating earlier fears.

2008

We went into the year with great expectations. The business was great early on, but it did not last. The Dow opened at 11,244, but it began dropping, and I was at a loss as to what to do. Interest rates climbed. The prime rate went to 8 percent.

An opportunity came up to buy out the franchise we had in Creve Coeur, for $600,000, and we elected to go for it. It increased our bank debt substantially, but the projected increase in profit more than offset the interest expenses on the loan.

In March, a long-standing financial institution, Bear Stearns, was on the brink of bankruptcy. JP Morgan took charge and bought the firm, but not after the collapse had shocked the country and the world. The market dropped again.

Kim and I had a meeting with Sam Garanzini and John Harris to come up with a plan, and we began to seriously watch the day-to-day receipts at all the stores, including the franchises.

Sales were slipping daily, not too much early on. But every time there was a drop in the market, the bad news by the media caused the drop excessively.

Real estate values began dropping at an alarming rate. Pres. George Bush and his financial people were meeting daily, trying to settle the country's nerves. But the panic grew worse, and the news media was not helping matters. Rumors were not helping either.

The credit markets were frozen, making it impossible to borrow money.

The government did a $700 billion bailout to help banks, forcing the big ones to borrow at almost zero interest.

And then Lehman Brothers filed bankruptcy and set off a global recession! Because of the drop in real estate, Freddie Mac and Fannie Mae were propped up by the government with a bailout of $187 billion! Again in an effort to lower interest rates, the government bought $800 billion in mortgage-backed securities.

All this activity had a serious negative effect on people in general. Businesses were feeling the pain as we were, and it seemed like the economy had come to a screeching halt.

Layoffs began taking effect even among the strongest firms, and we started losing some of our franchise stores. They simply did not have the financial strength to deal with the slowdown in business and closed the doors, and this affected our cash flow.

In November Barack Obama was elected president of the country, defeating Sen. John McCain of Arizona. This was a pause in the crazy disastrous economy, but the decline continued. The Dow closed down 34 percent at 8,816.

At the advice of my broker, I stayed the course and made no serious moves in the market. Fortunately, I was not on margin, so I lost nothing.

Kim came up with an interesting advertising campaign, using a good sales promotion, and it helped. But the economy was scaring people, even those who had steady employment, and the media was not helping. The nightly news was all about the disaster in the economy and the wars.

Because of the slowdown in daily sales, our vendors finally reached the point where they no longer would carry us for an extended period of time, and I had to loan money to the company to carry us and catch up with our accounts payable.

This also impacted our franchise income. By the end of the year, it dropped $75,000, some of the franchisees were having trouble paying us, and our reserve for bad debt went to $153,000.

We were forced to close our store in Chesterfield. This was a major letdown for us because it had been a winner. 2008 was another down year, and we closed in the red.

Our biggest concern was unemployment. It was at 5.8 percent early in the year, and by the first of 2009, it was 9 percent. Our business continued to drop.

Unemployment wreaked havoc on our business, and one by one we started closing stores. There was a fire at the franchise store in Fairview Heights, and we decided not to reopen it. We also closed the airport location in Concourse C; it was draining money every month. We ended the year with a sizable loss, and we decided to hold off any expansion until the economy returned to some sense of normalcy.

CHAPTER 13

2009

The dismal economy continued into 2009, and we were concerned about the new franchise store I was building in Union, Missouri. I told Kim to do everything he could regarding public relations. The new owner was being trained in our best store in St. Louis. Sam Garanzini was personally spending a lot of time with him to ensure he opened with the knowledge of what to expect from day one.

We had our best managers set to train the new hires for the new location weeks before the grand opening.

I was at the construction site every day, going back and forth from St. Louis, to ensure everything was on schedule for the opening. There was no room for error at any level.

We purposely set the opening on a normally slow day at our stores, so that we could put our entire management staff at the store for the grand opening.

Kim was meeting with the local newspaper and radio stations, buying ads in exchange for free publicity.

While all this was taking place, Kim suggested we get into the catering business. We had many requests to do weddings and corporate meetings, and we gave him the green light to set it up. Kim took charge of launching the new enterprise and put the word out to every major business in St. Louis and to suburban business leaders he knew.

The word spread quickly, and requests poured in immediately. We were not set up, and Sam quickly got his team together. In a matter of two weeks, he started this new phase of our business at a time when our regular store sales were declining due to the economy.

Kim came up with another idea at our weekly meeting, "Let's do a fast-food takeout business." He was approached by a developer to open a small store at the old post office downtown that was now a shopping center with a favorable lease, and we agreed to open later in the year. We called the new store Pasta House Pronto. It went over well initially, and we began looking for other locations that did not conflict with our current stores.

Unemployment continued to drop. The turmoil plagued the news every day. Banks that were in trouble were being sold every month. The FDIC was running out of money to support them. Thus, they began putting pressure on the bigger banks to buy them. The major banks were using cheap money they borrowed from the government to scoop up the small troubled banks.

That money was provided to lend to businesses to aid the recovery. This was contrary to the Fed's desire to help companies survive the disaster. Thus, two government agencies were fighting for the same dollars.

Meanwhile, the Dow Jones continued its decline, and the market suffered. Down from the opening in January at 8,885.65, it closed at the end of the year at 7,949.09, the lowest drop percentage-wise since 1890! Unemployment was at 10 percent at the end of the year. Our store-to-store business was off substantially, and our bank debt surged using our line of credit to aid cash flow to survive. It was close to $4 million.

We closed several stores: Branson, Missouri; Evansville; DeBaliviere; Belleville; and the franchise store in Alton, Illinois. There was no choice. They were bleeding money. But where possible from a seniority standpoint, we saved a few jobs and moved the top-performing people to existing stores. We also cut hours at most of the company stores to reduce our payroll. And so our corporate profit continued to slide, and we ended the year in the red.

2010

The bleak economy continued to dominate the news. Kim and I began to wonder whether things would ever get back to some semblance of normality. Some of the older stores were having trouble with various elements from a maintenance standpoint, and it started to weigh on me. I was spending 95 percent of my time going from store to store taking care of problems, and it was costing us serious money. From air conditioning to refrigeration to wear and tear on tables and chairs to light fixtures, there seemed no end to it.

The Federal Reserve continued to pour money into the economy, but it did not help very much, especially with regard to unemployment. While layoffs finally started to decline midyear, it was still high at 9.6 percent; it was estimated fifteen million people were out of work.

In September the government declared the recession was over. While things were getting better, certain parts of the country were still experiencing tough times, and that was the case in some of our areas.

As is always the case when the economy slows and there's excessive unemployment, crime raises its ugly head, and that was happening in some areas too.

We were forced to close Crestwood and the Pronto store at the old post office.

We struggled to pay the overhead and keep the doors open and ended up losing a substantial amount of money again. We continued to cut the staff, and Kim and I took pay cuts.

2011

Sam and Kim were pushing the catering business, and it was helping cash flow and profits.

It was the sole bright spot in our business. In the higher-income-per-capital areas, we started to see some light at the end of the tunnel.

One of the bright spots that seemed to take the economy off the minds of people in St. Louis was the Cardinals baseball team. They were having a good season and ended up in the World Series where they defeated the Texas Rangers in seven games.

For years Kim had been on my case to open a high-end Italian restaurant with our name. I fought him about it in 2008 and 2009, but in late 2010, I caved in and agreed.

We found a good location in Clayton where we were well known, and I spent a little over $700,000 building the store. In May of 2011, we opened Tucci and Fresta's, only after Kim had promised he would run it. It lasted two years! I have tried to forget this, but every time I drive by the location, it continues to haunt me. We converted it to a Pasta House to cover the lease and ultimately shut it down later when the lease term ran out.

The good news was we turned the previous three-year losses into a nice profit for the year.

2012

The presidential election for November began to dominate the news, but it continued to focus on the wars in Iraq and Afghanistan. The death toll on Americans fighting in the war exceeded two thousand! An attack on the US embassy in Benghazi, Libya, shook the world and put pressure on Secretary of State Hillary Clinton because of lack of security. Our ambassador to Libya was killed in the attack, and the media was all over this for weeks afterward.

Mitt Romney, the former Republican governor of Massachusetts, was nominated to run against President Obama in the November election. And on November 6, Obama easily defeated him.

The good news was unemployment dropped to 7.7 percent by the end of the year, but twelve million people were still estimated to be out of work.

We were once again facing reality that some of our choices regarding the financial stability of the people we chose to issue franchises to were not good, and we closed two stores. That, coupled with our slow sales late in the year, put us in the red for 2012.

2013

Kim and I decided to continue our conservative approach to every facet of our business. We advised Sam Garanzini and John Harris to continue to hold down payroll and food expenses and put pressure on John Harris to watch the general overhead in an effort to continue to reduce the bank debt.

Our cash flow continued the downfall, and I had to loan money for the company to stay open.

We also decided not to seek any new franchisees and open only company-owned stores.

Kim was doing a good job with the catering business and pushing public relations in all markets, and it showed in store-to-store business.

Unemployment was at 7 percent by the end of the year, and the recovery helped us to renew expansion. We knew we had the formula for success. Our years of experience, with contacts at every level of business, coupled with our management staff, had allowed us to weather many storms. And we had a bank that believed in us. Once again the loan at the bank increased to our limit.

We closed Joe's Chili Bowl. It was not officially on The Pasta House books. Kim and I owned it separately. It still cost us both money and took our time to deal with all the financial matters. However, the year's profits cheered us, for finally we ended in the black with a well-earned profit.

The year was highlighted by the St. Louis Cardinals playing in the World Series only to be defeated by the Boston Red Sox.

ITALIAN RESTAURANTS

CHAPTER 14

2014, Kim Tucci

Once again it seemed like there was no end to the dark clouds hovering above our heads. Every time we weathered a disaster and returned to some semblance of normalcy, *boom!* We got jolted with a thunderbolt!

Kim was not feeling well, and I kept urging him to go see his doctor. I am sure he sensed something serious was hanging over him, and he waved me off, almost to the point where I felt I was bothering him. So I stopped. He and John Harris had been working closely together, and John tried to reason with him.

Finally, he made an appointment to visit the doctor, who immediately put him through a series of tests. And we learned after the results came back that his cancer returned!

It first attacked his prostate, and the biopsy confirmed the prognosis. While he was being treated, the discomfort was having a bad effect on him, but he tolerated the pain.

Then the unexpected happened. The cancer attacked his knee replacement, and it was necessary to remove the replaced knee, forcing him into rehab and a wheelchair.

Later his pacemaker was attacked, and it was removed. As the year progressed, he was so disabled he hardly showed up at the office.

There was no doubt his role was to be limited in the business, and for years he was in and out of the hospital.

On August 9, Michael Brown was shot in Ferguson, Missouri, by a police officer at the site of one of our stores. It became major national news across the country.

Looting and rioting in most urban areas were rampant, and Ferguson was the epicenter. We were expecting our store to be burned down and had made the decision not to reopen if it happened. For some reason, it was spared, whereas almost every major business in town suffered serious damage.

Meanwhile, the economy had not fully recovered, even though unemployment had dropped to 5.9 percent. Our business was still struggling, and bank debt continued to escalate.

We opened two more Pronto stores, one in Kirkwood, Missouri, a well-established suburb of St. Louis, and another on Brentwood Boulevard in Clayton. Both did well initially.

In 2015, I received a call from a gentleman with regard to a location in St. Charles, Missouri, another St. Louis suburb northwest of the city. And after checking out the site, I agreed to build a store there. It was the first major expansion since the recession.

I was juggling a few balls. With Kim's illness, everyone in the company was tugging at my time. Store managers were calling me with maintenance problems at all hours of the day and night.

Sam was at me when food supplies were not arriving on time from Italy. John Harris was also at me when we were short of cash. He presented bad news regarding three of the franchises that were not paying their fees, and we decided to close all three of them by the end of the year. Once again we lost money for the year.

I had taken over Kim's role with regard to the catering business. Most of his other responsibilities were shared by Sam Garanzini and John Harris. The pressure was on all of us.

Meanwhile, Kim was in and out of the hospital the entire year, and I was there to visit him every day in an effort to assure him he was going to beat the cancer. But he was down. He kept saying, "All I want to do is die." I kept telling him, "Don't talk like that." The situation was wearing me down psychologically. I kept asking myself,

"Why Kim? Why not me?" What did he do to deserve this? He was not living; he was existing. We all knew it was a matter of time before he would pass.

2015

The year was highlighted by the number of people opting for the nominations on the part of both parties for the presidency in the 2016 election. Hillary Clinton announced early that she was running again for the Democratic nomination. And as the year unfolded, sixteen Republicans announced, including Donald Trump.

Our business at our store again was disrupted because a man shot two city policemen in front of the Ferguson police headquarters.

The good news was low interest rates were helping us with our bank loans and unemployment dropped to 5 percent, and that helped increase our business.

We slashed our overhead dramatically, Sam Garanzini did an incredible job reducing food costs, the franchises did the same, and we all took pay cuts and turned things around and finally showed a huge profit for the year.

In 2016, we followed up with a long-discussed franchise in Festus, Missouri. And to this day that year is a blur. I don't know where I had the time to do everything, but somehow with the help of our great well-trained management team, we got the store open in record time. That store is still open today.

The other stores, both company-owned and franchises, were operating at record levels. John Harris was presenting me with daily success numbers as to cash flow, bank debt, and profit and loss statements, which I brought to Kim on my visits in an effort to cheer him up. But it was not helping for he was in constant pain. The negative effect haunted me and was constantly on my mind.

I spoke to his doctor on numerous occasions, and finally one day, he assured me they were doing all they could do to keep him comfortable. And then I had the courage to ask him, "Is he going to make it?" and the doctor replied with his head down and just shook his head. He could not get the words out!

As the year progressed, we opened another franchise store on Weidman Road in another suburb of St. Louis. Once again The Pasta House team rose to the occasion, and we opened right on time. That store also is open today and continues to aid the growth in revenue for the company.

Business continued to rise, and the only negative was Kim's cancer. It continued to concern us. By now he was in the hospital for lengthy stays. I was there daily, and he shocked me one day by asking me, "Bring me a gun so I can blow my brains out."

What do you say to a guy who has been your close friend and business partner for over thirty years? My feelings for him, his pain and discomfort, and the mental anguish he was experiencing were out of control.

I had nothing left emotionally, no words in my vocabulary to ease his pain. I was suffering the defeatist attitude with him. I tried to put myself in his shoes, wondering how I would react if it was me lying in that bed, and had to jolt myself back to reality. I could not allow him to see me like this. It became a major effort to get myself to that hospital every day, for no matter how hard I tried, I would leave depressed, helpless with no more encouraging words to share with him. Kim was a bright guy, and he could read through BS, so I stopped trying to prop him up. It was useless.

The election was occupying the news, and Secretary of State Hillary Clinton was seeking the Democratic nomination for president, and several noted Republicans had announced their hope to win the nomination for the coming November election.

Donald Trump began moving ahead of the Republicans, seeking the nomination, and it was getting heated during the debates. The established politicians attacked Trump, but he was holding his own and drawing major attention from the TV commentators across all networks.

One by one most of those opposed to him started dropping out after his leads in the primaries, and Trump succeeded in winning the nomination.

Now Hillary began attacking Trump and initially taking an early lead in the polls. As the election day was nearing, she led in most polls for the Democratic-dominated states.

Trump was drawing huge crowds and campaigning vigorously and ended up taking the major states with larger electoral votes, winning the election and becoming the forty-fifth president of the country.

We ended the year with record earnings, making up the losses for the previous years! We moved our corporate offices to a new facility on Ballas Road, and I sold the building at the old place on Macklind Avenue.

In 2017 Kim's body was racked with cancer. Drugs were keeping him alive. He was in and out of the hospital most of the year. I was having trouble sleeping. Phyllis and I would be in nice restaurants, and all I could think about was Kim eating hospital food and here we were in a fine setting, dining on gourmet food. The food was no longer a factor. All I wanted to do was get home and watch TV to get my mind off everything.

My mental capacity was occupied, trying to figure out what would happen when my good friend passed. We were inseparable. I spent more time with him during the week than with my wife. What was going to happen to the business? He was the mainstay.

I was not concerned for myself but the employees, and Sam and John were dominating my mind. I was seventy-eight years old. Our key people had been with the company for decades. We employed over 250 people.

Friends kept telling me, "Joe, take it one day at a time. Make sure he is not suffering. He would want you to stay the course, not to worry about him. Take care of the business."

Thanks to the dedication of Sam and John and the well-trained staff at every level, we showed a nice profit again in 2017.

CHAPTER 15

Succession

2018 was uneventful. My mind was not on the business. I left the day-to-day operation to Sam and John. I had trouble concentrating on anything but Kim and the day-to-day ups and downs with his illness. He and I had discussions about his life. I no longer tried to discuss it or attempt to get him "up." It was useless. I tried to go back over the years, especially some of the disasters that had become laughable, and once in a while he would smile. That strategy was not working.

Next, the food at the hospital was barely edible. That prompted me to have Sam prepare lunch and dinner for him, with me bringing it to the hospital, but he would take a few bites and push it away. His weight was down, and it showed in his face. He was not the same guy.

We had put expansion on the back burner, and no stores were opened that year. There was some concern about the stock market. Even that had no effect on me. I had stopped watching the day-to-day activity. I was focused on Kim. Period. I was walking around in a daze. The entire year is a blur. Every time I walked out of the hospital, I wondered whether it would be the last time I saw him alive.

I would drive home and not remember the route I took to get there. At times I would forget to go to the restaurant where I had agreed to meet Phyllis for dinner, only to receive a call from her, saying, "Where are you? I am at the restaurant. Did you forget?"

This was worse than all the traumas we had experienced the entire time we had been together.

And I often had a talk with myself to be reminded that my good friend was the one suffering.

Once in a while Sam or John would discuss an inquiry from someone regarding a franchise, or a call would come in from a realtor or shopping center developer, and I told them to put it off for now. There was no way I wanted to even think about building a new store.

In my daily visits, Kim seemed to go down a little every day. It was obvious now. His time was limited. We both ran out of words to say. I would sit there for hours without uttering a word. He would nod off to sleep, the drugs sedating him. When he was awake, lying there silently, I continued to wonder what he was thinking.

Once in a while, he would ask how things were going, and I tried to discuss the status with the business to get his mind off his condition. But before I could finish, he would nod off right in the middle of the discussion. It was torture.

To this day, sometimes at night, I wake and have trouble going back to sleep. And my mind drifts back to some of our conversations, especially in the early days when there was no doubt in his mind or mine that his days were numbered.

The tension and stress of dealing with this really were controlling my emotions. I was so wrought with the situation that my normal easygoing personality was reaching a breaking point, and at times with store managers and John and Sam, I had to control my temper.

My stockbroker called one day and told me the market was down substantially, and I told him not to bother me about the market. Later I called him back and apologized. He knew about Kim, and he apologized back to me.

Once in a while, Phyllis tried to get my mind off the status by discussing something regarding our boys or some event in the news, and it had little effect on me—especially things politically.

I tried to watch the news on occasion, but I could not concentrate. When the market crashed in December, I took the posture if I don't sell, I have not lost anything. I could care less.

2019

At the hospital in early March, the doctor was in Kim's room when I arrived, and he and I had a talk in the hall outside Kim's room. He informed me it could be any day. Kim was so sedated that I sat there most of the day and we did not exchange two words. I could read his mind. He knew the situation.

I remember that day like it was yesterday. I thought about one of our most memorable days, when he said, "Joe, I know I'm not going to make it. I am ready for that day. But I feel good that you will be able to keep things going. We are lucky to have well-trained people. You have been a great partner, a great friend, and I love you."

Kim Tucci passed away on March 25, a day forever indelible on my mind. He was seventy-eight. I was at home when I received the call. There is no way to describe my emotions. I tried to understand why. Again, why him and not me? I remember talking to Joe Reina one day and I asked him that question and he had a simple answer, "Joe, your time is not up. You still have things to do in this world. When it's your time, the guy upstairs will call for you!"

The funeral was held at the St. Louis Cathedral Basilica. Every top business person, politician, media person, and a close friend attended. Over two thousand were there. It was standing room only both inside and outside.

Kim was honored by dozens of nonprofits and St. Louis organizations over the years.

When things finally returned to some semblance of normality, we settled with Kim's estate, and our key man insurance put that to rest.

It finally dawned on me. It was me now. I thanked Sam and John for their joint effort in 2018 and the final days in 2019 for taking charge of the business. They were doing Kim's job and, for the most part, mine.

It was the end of an era. I would occasionally sit in my office and think back over the years, the ups and downs, the challenges we overcame, successes and failures. I tried to recall how many stores I built and lost count after sixty-five and estimated we spent over $50 million. The sad news was most have closed over the years.

I reminded myself, "I am still here. And I am lucky to be alive, with numerous things to be grateful for, starting with Phyllis, my boys, and the loyal employees, especially John and Sam. I have nothing to complain about. I have a business to run." All those people just mentioned were counting on me to continue down the path we chartered in 1974. They had a life with house payments, car payments, and kids in college. They worked hard over the years to afford me the lifestyle Phyllis and I enjoyed. It was time to go to work. That's what Kim would want me to do.

There was an echo from him in my mind, "Carry the ball, Joe."

All that sounded good, but while I accepted the fact he was gone physically, emotionally I was a mess. All those years, the efforts to keep his spirits up, and living with him day after day took their toll. I would go to the office early in the morning and spend time with Sam and John on operations and financial matters, but by eleven most days, there was nothing for me to do. I scheduled lunches with friends, and they tried to console me in good faith. All it did was bring back the anguish. I knew 2019 was going to be another blur, and that's what it turned out to be.

We used to talk four or five times a day on the phone when we did not see each other, and I miss that.

ITALIAN RESTAURANTS

CHAPTER 16

It's Just Me Now

2020–2021

John Harris and Sam were a tremendous help in keeping my head up in the early days after Kim's passing. We met every day, and I learned what I had been missing on the day-to-day activities while spending time at the hospital. Those two guys were running the show.

Sam informed me we had been approached by a man who had several urgent care establishments throughout the city and suburbs and he wanted to buy out the lease of our Delmar store. I immediately said, "That is not going to happen."

This was the site of the original Rich and Charlie's. There was a sentimental feeling about it, to say nothing of the fact that our business was great. It was a neighborhood hangout, with steady customers, and there was no way I was going to let it close.

The guy kept raising the price he was willing to pay, and John and Sam finally convinced me it was the right move, and we could use the money to pay down the bank debt.

I found a location just two miles from the store. While it was half the size, I caved in, and we made the move. It was a restaurant that had shut down, and I spent less than $200,000 to turn it into a Pasta House, and it continues to be a good store for us to this day.

The pandemic rocked the nation in the middle of March, and the city and county shut us down. I had to lay off two hundred people, and it severely affected our business as was the case for most businesses. I cut the staff to four or five people in each store, and we started advertising takeout and curb service, and it immediately sparked the business.

My attitude was people still have to eat.

Before long we received a PPP loan from the government. And it, too, helped save us. We shared that money with the people we laid off and those who had stayed the course with us.

By fall when the number of new cases subsided, we were allowed to reopen. But with severe restrictions, the customers who entered had to wear a mask until their food arrived. Due to keeping the tables six feet apart, we were limited to 25 percent capacity. The good news was our takeout and curb street business continued, and once again like a cat with nine lives, we dodged another trauma and survived.

We had to deal with the problems most companies were dealing with: food shortages and people getting sick and failing to show up for work. Masking and distancing took their toll and tested our patience. Our customers were very generous with tipping our curbside employees, and it did wonders for the morale.

And so it ends, a survival of the fittest. Never in my early education did I dream that "term" would play such a dramatic part in my life. As a child going on picnics at the Forest Park Highlands amusement park, I used to love riding the roller coaster; it was scary. But it was nothing compared to the one that has impacted my life the past forty-seven years!

But here I am, the sole survivor of a success story of a dream had by a bunch of guys from The Hill. Sandwiched in the dream were a few nightmares.

I am grateful for being blessed with the experiences and the employees we have, too many to name. But I would be remiss not to mention Sam Garanzini and John Harris for their loyalty, dedication, integrity, and friendship.

ITALIAN RESTAURANTS

EPILOGUE

In 1973 when Kim and I opened our Rich and Charlie's franchise in Ballwin, my wife, Phyllis, and I had been married for ten years and were raising two boys, Joe and Paul.

Being a successful restaurant owner is hard work: long hours, eighteen-hour days, seven days a week, to say nothing of the stress associated with it.

It involves the constant support of one's wife and family.

Phyllis kept the household and family activities running smoothly, reminding me of important family activities that needed my attention and attendance.

She is my soul mate and partner in life.

This year, 2022, is our fifty-ninth anniversary and our fiftieth year in the restaurant business. I would be lost without her. We both agree the success of my business and our lives together is our love for each other and our love for our family.

And so the story of the last man standing comes to an end. Looking back, the fifty years are a blur. Where did the time go? Here I am, the sole survivor of the wild ride of ups and downs, successes, and failures of a bunch of guys from The Hill, who had a dream that became reality.

I bless the people who rode the roller coaster along with me. The best was Phyllis. Never once did she suggest throwing in the towel. There are too many others to mention. I owe tremendous gratitude and thanks to everyone.

While I have had some serious downtimes and laid awake many nights, I would not trade the experience for anything in the world.

I have had the pleasure of meeting people from all walks of life, from every profession, and I have learned so much from the experience.

There are no words in my vocabulary to express the warm feelings I have for those who helped put me in the place I enjoy today. I no longer question why I enjoy the pleasure of owning the business alone. The partners are gone, but their spirits continue to hover over the business. Not a day goes by that some reminder surfaces and I am reminded they are still with me.

Paul Fresta and Joe Fresta Jr., Down to Two

Joe and Phyllis Fresta

Joe Fresta and Mother Pauline Caputa Scuito

ITALIAN RESTAURANTS

ABOUT THE AUTHORS

Joe Reina was born of Sicilian immigrants in St. Louis, Missouri, on February 7, 1936. He attended Shaw Grade School and graduated from Southwest High School. He began working at the Arrow Shirt company in September 1954 while taking night classes at St. Louis University. Later, as a salesman for Arrow, he was promoted to district manager in the firm's Chicago office in 1970. He continued his education for three years, taking night classes at Northwestern University.

While in Chicago to hedge against excessive income tax, Joe ventured into real estate. Throughout his adult life, most of his business career kept him involved in the apparel industry. It required international travel and enabled him to explore a good part of the world. Joe is the author of *The Goat Sleeps in the Kitchen*, *Italy Under My Skin*, and *Giancarlo Giambrone*.

Joe is retired and lives in Scottsdale, Arizona.

* * * * *

Joe Fresta, a native St. Louisian, transitioned from working as a carpenter to owning restaurants. He brought his skills as a carpenter with him, helping to develop a successful restaurant chain, The Pasta House Company. Joe and his wife, Phyllis, have two sons, Joe Junior and Paul, and a granddaughter, Sabrina. *Molte grazie* to Joe Reina who coauthored this book with him.

CPSIA information can be obtained
at www.ICGtesting.com
Printed in the USA
JSHW082037271122
33811JS00002B/6

9 781685 267964